W9-AZO-287

WITHDRAWN

Building Greenscrapers

by Steven L. Stern

Consultant: Frank Robbins, LEED AP
(Leadership in Energy and Environmental Design,
Accredited Professional)

BEARPORT

PORTER MEMORIAL BRANCH LIBRARY
NEWTON COUNTY LIBRARY SYSTEM
6191 HIGHWAY 212
COVINGTON, GA 30016

Credits

Cover and Title Page, © Robin O'Connell/iStockphoto; 4-5, © Nancy Louie/iStockphoto; 6, © Alina Hart/iStockphoto; 7, © Christopher Arndt/iStockphoto; 9T, Courtesy of IWS/Watercache.com; 9M, © Tim Graham/Getty Images; 9B, © Rob Melnychuk/Digital Vision/Alamy; 10L, © Morgan Lane Photography/iStockphoto; 10R, © Hal_P/Shutterstock; 11, © Nic Lehoux/Nic Lehoux Photographie Architecturale; 12, © A. T. Willett/Alamy; 13, © Steve Dunwell/Photographer's Choice/Getty Images; 15, © AP Images/Chicago Department of Environment/Mark Farina; 17, Courtesy of Solarcentury.com/Yan Preston; 18, © Terrance Emerson/Shutterstock; 19, Courtesy of Atkins; 21, Courtesy of KMD Architects; 22, © Gordon Graff; 23, Courtesy of MAD Architectural Design Office, Beijing, China; 24, © Chuck Choi/Arcaid/Corbis; 25, Courtesy of UCX Architects/Vestia Rotterdam Feijenoord; 26, Courtesy of Gerber Architekten International; 27, © LVM Group Inc./via Bloomberg News./Landov; 28, Courtesy of Skidmore, Owings & Merrill LLP; 29, © Markus Gann/Shutterstock.

Publisher: Kenn Goin
Editorial Director: Adam Siegel
Creative Director: Spencer Brinker
Photo Researcher: Jennifer Bright

The Going Green series is printed on recycled paper.

Library of Congress Cataloging-in-Publication Data

Stern, Steven L.
  Building greenscrapers / by Steven L. Stern ; consultant, Frank Robbins.
    p. cm. — (Going green)
  Includes bibliographical references and index.
  ISBN-13: 978-1-59716-962-2 (library binding)
  ISBN-10: 1-59716-962-5 (library binding)
  1. Skyscrapers—Environmental aspects—Juvenile literature. 2. Sustainable buildings—Juvenile literature. 3. Building—Environmental aspects—Juvenile literature. I. Robbins, Frank, consultant. II. Title.

TH1615.S74 2010
720'.47—dc22

                    2009012494

Copyright © 2010 Bearport Publishing Company, Inc. All rights reserved. No part of this publication may be reproduced in whole or in part, stored in a retrieval system, or transmitted in any form or by any means, electronic, mechanical, photocopying, recording, or otherwise, without written permission from the publisher.

For more information, write to Bearport Publishing Company, Inc., 101 Fifth Avenue, Suite 6R, New York, New York 10003. Printed in the United States of America.

10 9 8 7 6 5 4 3 2 1

Contents

What Is a "Greenscraper"?

Millions of people around the world live and work in skyscrapers. With their awesome height and dramatic architecture, these soaring buildings make cities exciting places to visit and explore.

Skyscrapers, however, also create many problems. Large amounts of **natural resources** are needed to build them. Then, after they're built, lots of energy is needed to keep their lights, heating and cooling systems, and computers operating.

Luckily, builders are finding ways to make skyscrapers "green"—that is, more **energy efficient** and friendly toward the environment. These greenscrapers, as green skyscrapers are sometimes called, **conserve** energy and water. They also provide better indoor air for people who work or live in them and release less pollution outside than traditional skyscrapers. Greenscrapers use the latest **technology** to serve people's needs without harming Earth.

Philadelphia's skyscrapers

The word *skyscraper* first meant the sail at the top of a ship's tall mast. In the late 1800s, though, people began using the word to describe buildings that seemed to touch the sky.

Using Recycled Materials

Skyscrapers are made out of concrete, steel, and other materials. Making buildings from these materials uses up a lot of natural resources that are in **limited** supply. For example, steel is made from iron ore, which has to be mined from the ground. Once Earth's supply of iron ore is used up, there won't be any left—so people have to use it carefully.

To conserve Earth's resources, greenscrapers are built with **recycled** materials. For example, each year millions of tons of steel from old cans and from cars, refrigerators, and other machines are melted to make new steel. Using this recycled steel reduces waste, since the old steel that would have been thrown away is now used to make new steel.

Steel beams and columns form the frame, or "skeleton," of a skyscraper. Concrete is then poured around these supporting pieces.

The Sears Tower

It takes a lot of steel to make a skyscraper. When it was built in 1973, the Sears Tower (now called the Willis Tower) needed about 76,000 tons (68,946 metric tons) of steel. That's enough to make 50,000 cars!

Besides steel, other recycled materials are also used in modern skyscrapers. For example, recycled plastic may be used to make carpeting, ceiling tiles, and even some furniture.

Saving Water

Freshwater is precious. People need it not only for drinking but also for washing, cooking, and growing food. Unfortunately, 97 percent of Earth's water is salty and cannot be used for these purposes. The remaining 3 percent is freshwater, but less than 1 percent of it can be collected, stored, and piped to communities. The rest is frozen in glaciers and other giant pieces of ice. Since such a small amount of the world's water can be used by people, it is important not to waste it.

To use less piped-in water, a greenscraper collects rainwater on its roof and stores it in large tanks. The rainwater can then be used in the building's toilets and cooling system. People also use it to water gardens and plants around the building. In some greenscrapers, rainwater supplies half of the water a building needs.

Faucets, toilets, and other bathroom fixtures designed to reduce water flow are also helping people conserve water. The "low-flow" fixtures use about half as much water as regular fixtures.

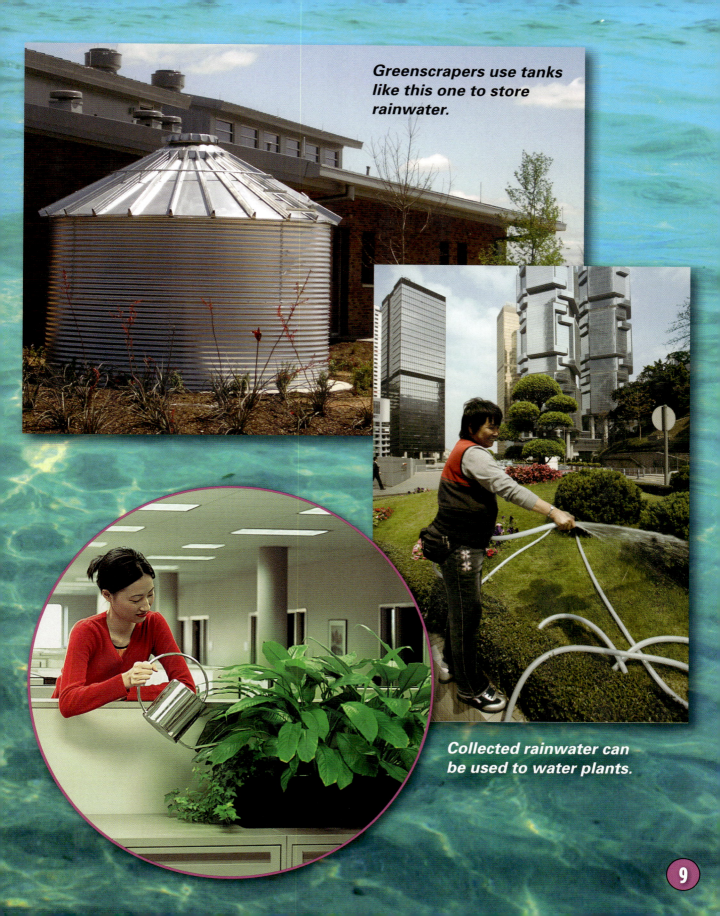

Greenscrapers use tanks like this one to store rainwater.

Collected rainwater can be used to water plants.

Using Light Wisely

People need light to do their work. Unfortunately, all the burning lightbulbs inside a skyscraper use a lot of energy. In fact, nearly 30 percent of the energy consumed in offices, homes, schools, and other buildings goes for lighting.

To reduce the amount of energy used for this purpose, people in greenscrapers are replacing **incandescent lightbulbs** with **compact fluorescent lightbulbs** (CFLs). These bulbs use less electricity and last longer. Some buildings even use LEDs, or light-emitting diodes. These tiny electric light-producing devices are expensive, but they use less energy and last up to ten times longer than CFLs.

An incandescent lightbulb (left) and an energy-efficient CFL (right)

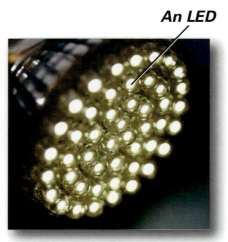

An LED

In some greenscrapers, computers and light **sensors** control the lighting to save electricity. As sunlight streams through windows, sensors automatically dim the lights. Sensors can also detect people and their movements. If all the people in a room leave without turning out the lights, the sensors do the job for them.

Glass-walled offices in the 52-story New York Times building allow natural light to come in. The greenscraper's lighting-control system has reduced electrical lighting use by 70 percent.

Heating and Cooling

Greenscrapers and other buildings use energy to heat air in the winter and cool it in the summer. To keep heated or cooled air from escaping—and energy from being wasted—builders put **insulation** within the buildings' walls and roofs.

The most common insulation material is **fiberglass**. This fluffy, cotton-like substance is made of fine threads of glass that have been bonded together. The thicker the fiberglass, the better the insulation.

Fiberglass being installed

Greenscrapers also have double- and triple-pane windows to stop heat from leaking out of them. These windows are made with two or three sheets of glass instead of only one. In one of the newest kinds of windows, a special gas called argon fills the space between panes. On cold days, the gas acts as an insulator, preventing heat from escaping.

Some greenscrapers use computerized climate-control systems. These systems monitor inside and outside temperatures and automatically adjust heating and cooling to save energy.

Gardens in the Sky

Some greenscrapers are topped with green roofs—roofs covered with grass, flowers, shrubs, and even trees. These rooftop gardens are more than just beautiful to look at. They are also good for the environment.

Cities crammed with buildings, paved streets, and sidewalks have hotter temperatures than surrounding areas. Heat from the sun is absorbed by these structures and surfaces, and it builds up to create what's called a **heat island effect**. The result is that cities may be several degrees warmer than their surroundings during the day and up to 22°F (12°C) warmer at night.

Green roofs reduce the heat island effect. In the summer, they block the sun's heat with cooling shade—which cuts air-conditioning costs and saves energy. In the winter, the garden's layer of soil provides insulation, helping to keep heat inside the building—and saving more energy.

Green roofs help to improve air quality in cities. Plants produce oxygen and consume carbon dioxide—a gas that traps heat in the atmosphere and adds to **global warming**. Plants also clean the air, removing tiny pieces of dirt that contribute to **smog**.

Older buildings can also become green. In 2000, a rooftop garden (shown below) was added to the top of Chicago's City Hall—an 11-story office building that was completed in 1911. The garden has more than 20,000 plants.

Energy from the Sun

It takes a lot of electricity to run a skyscraper. The electricity is needed not just for lighting but also to run computers, refrigerators, air conditioners, and many other machines. However, most of the **generators** that produce electric power are themselves powered by burning oil, coal, or gas. At the rate people are using these **fuels**, they will run out someday. Also, the fuels give off gases that **pollute** the air when they are burned.

To help solve these problems, greenscrapers are using technology to capture the sun's energy. **Solar panels** can turn sunlight into electricity. These thin, flat panels contain many **solar cells**. When sunlight falls on solar cells, they produce electrical power.

Placing solar panels on greenscrapers cuts down on the amount of fuel that a building uses. What's more, solar panels are powered by something that will not run out—the sun—and they do not cause pollution.

Solar panels won't work at night or on cloudy days, but they can be connected to rechargeable batteries. These batteries store some of the energy collected on sunny days for later use.

This skyscraper in England is covered with 7,000 solar panels.

Wind Power

Sunlight is not the only source of energy that will not run out or pollute the air. Some greenscrapers use the power of the wind to make electricity. They do this by using **wind turbines**.

A wind turbine looks a little like a fan, but the way it works is the opposite. A fan uses electricity to produce wind. A turbine uses wind to produce electricity. The wind turns the blades of the turbine, which are connected to a generator.

Wind turbines may be placed on the roof of a building or attached to the side. Some greenscrapers use both solar panels and wind turbines. Together, these features can help buildings meet many of their power needs.

Sometimes large numbers of wind turbines are grouped together on land or in the water to form "wind farms" that produce electricity. One of the largest wind farms in the world is in Texas. It has 421 wind turbines that generate enough electricity to power 220,000 homes per year.

Wind turbines in California

The 95-foot (29-m) blades on these giant wind turbines produce one-tenth of the energy needed by the Bahrain World Trade Center. The building is located in Bahrain, a country in the Persian Gulf.

A Breath of Fresh Air

Ventilation systems replace indoor air with outdoor air. Drawing in fresh air from outside improves the air quality for people who live or work in buildings. The flow of fresh air can also lower the temperature in warm rooms, making people more comfortable.

Natural ventilation saves energy by refreshing and cooling the air inside a building without using electricity. Opening windows is one way to bring in fresh air. However, some greenscrapers have built-in structures that cause air to flow naturally through the buildings.

One example is the **thermal chimney**, a ventilation shaft that lets warm air flow out of a building. This movement takes place because warm air is lighter than cold air and naturally rises. As the warm air moves up through the chimney, vents located at the building's lower levels allow cooler outside air to flow into the building to take the place of the warm air.

How a Thermal Chimney Works

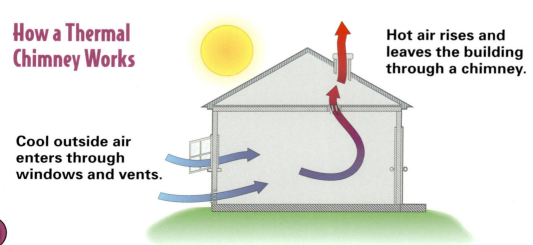

Hot air rises and leaves the building through a chimney.

Cool outside air enters through windows and vents.

This 12-story greenscraper will be one of San Francisco's newest office towers. A combination of solar panels and wind turbines will provide 40 percent of the building's energy needs, and a thermal chimney will help keep people cool inside.

Too little ventilation in a building can be bad for a person's health. People who live or work in a poorly ventilated building may experience headaches as well as eye, nose, or throat problems.

Dazzling Designs

Architects around the world are using their imaginations to design greenscrapers that use resources wisely. For example, the Hearst Tower in New York City has a frame of triangular shapes that lets in more natural light than normal windows.

The Sinosteel International Plaza building, being built in China, features a honeycomb pattern of windows. This beehive-like arrangement saves energy because windows of different sizes have been carefully placed to allow just the right amount of light and heat inside.

One of the most unusual design ideas that architects have imagined is a farming skyscraper. Such a building would combine living areas with spaces for growing vegetables or grain. A "sky farm" could provide food for many people—while giving new meaning to the term "greenscraper."

An architect's vision of a sky farm

The Sinosteel International Plaza will be completed in 2012.

Architects are exploring ways to make older skyscrapers greener. One possibility is to attach structures along the outside of buildings to hold wind turbines or gardens.

Just the Facts

Greenscrapers are being built around the world. Here are six of them.

The Hearst Tower: New York City

The 46-story Hearst Tower is New York's first greenscraper. This office building was completed in 2006.

- The Hearst Tower uses the outside of a building completed in 1928 as its base.

- More than 80 percent of the steel used to construct the greenscraper was recycled. The building's floors and ceiling tiles are also made from recycled materials.

- Rainwater is collected on the roof. From there, it is piped into a 14,000-gallon (52,996-l) tank in the building's basement. Enough water is collected to meet 50 percent of the building's water needs.

- Light sensors keep track of the natural light coming in and automatically adjust the amount of electric lighting.

- Motion sensors automatically turn off lights in empty offices after everyone leaves.

- Chemically-coated glass helps keep out the sun's heat so the inside of the building will stay cooler in hot weather. The treated glass reduces the need for air-conditioning and saves energy.

The Urban Cactus: Rotterdam, Netherlands

This unusual greenscraper really does look like a cactus! It is an apartment building that is being designed for the waterfront in Rotterdam, the Netherlands's second-largest city.

- The planned building will have 19 floors and almost 100 apartments. Each apartment will have an outdoor balcony for gardening. When the gardens are in bloom, this building truly will be a *green*scraper!

- The alternating arrangement of curved balconies will allow apartments on each floor to get large amounts of sunshine. It will also allow the gardens to be watered by rainfall.

- The building's white color will reflect, or bounce back, light, which will reduce the heat island effect.

- The architects hope to include solar panels and a water collection system as part of the building design.

Burj al-Taqa:
Dubai, United Arab Emirates

This skyscraper is being designed to have many green features.

- The building, which will be built in a hot climate, is shaped like a cylinder to limit the amount of surface exposed to the sun. Special glass reduces the amount of heat that enters through windows.

- A 197-foot (60-m) wind turbine will be located on the roof.

- About 160,000 square feet (14,864 sq m) of solar panels will also be located on the roof. More energy will be provided by a large group of solar panels that will float in the water near the skyscraper.

- The solar panels and wind turbine will generate enough electricity to meet the building's needs.

- Mirrors on the roof will reflect sunlight into the center of the building to provide natural light to the inside of the skyscraper.

An artist's drawing of Burj al-Taqa

Bank of America Tower: New York City

This 54-story high-rise office building is about 1,200 feet (366 m) tall. One of New York's newest greenscrapers, it is designed to use only half as much energy and water as a typical office building.

- The building is constructed mainly out of recycled materials. For example, all the steel used for support columns is recycled from scrap metal.

- The building collects, stores, and reuses rainwater and wastewater. Bathrooms have water-saving plumbing fixtures. As a result, the building will save millions of gallons (liters) of water each year.

- Floor-to-ceiling windows let in plenty of light. The glass is insulated to keep heat inside the building during cold weather.

- To save electricity, sensors automatically dim or brighten lights as needed. LED lighting also helps reduce energy use.

- There are many gardens within the skyscraper to improve indoor air quality.

The Pearl River Tower: Guangzhou, China

(Skidmore, Owings & Merrill LLP, archt.)

Shaped like a giant wing, this 71-story building will rise 1,017 feet (310 m) into the air. It is expected to use approximately 60 percent less energy than the typical Chinese office building. When construction is completed in 2010, the Pearl River Tower will be one of the world's greenest skyscrapers.

- Four wind turbines built into two floors of the skyscraper will provide electricity for the building.

- The building's unusual curved shape is designed to push air through the turbines. This design more than doubles the wind's speed. The faster speed makes the turbines generate even more power.

- The building will include a rainwater collection system. Some of the water collected will be heated by the sun to make hot water.

- Solar panels will help to provide electricity for the building.

- Automatic window blinds will open or close depending on the position of the sun.

- Insulated, chemically-coated glass will help to keep out the sun's heat.

An artist's drawing of the Pearl River Tower

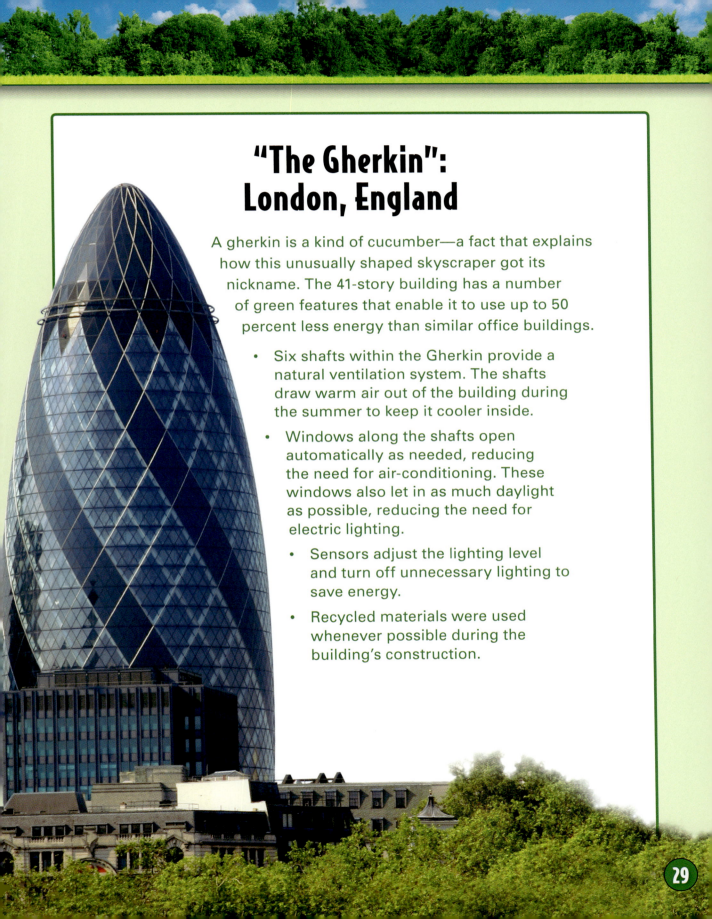

"The Gherkin": London, England

A gherkin is a kind of cucumber—a fact that explains how this unusually shaped skyscraper got its nickname. The 41-story building has a number of green features that enable it to use up to 50 percent less energy than similar office buildings.

- Six shafts within the Gherkin provide a natural ventilation system. The shafts draw warm air out of the building during the summer to keep it cooler inside.

- Windows along the shafts open automatically as needed, reducing the need for air-conditioning. These windows also let in as much daylight as possible, reducing the need for electric lighting.

  - Sensors adjust the lighting level and turn off unnecessary lighting to save energy.

  - Recycled materials were used whenever possible during the building's construction.

Everyone can play a part in "living green." Here are some things that people can do even if they don't live or work in a skyscraper:

- When incandescent lightbulbs burn out, replace them with CFLs (compact fluorescent lightbulbs). Replacing just one incandescent lightbulb in every home in America with an energy-efficient CFL would save enough energy to light more than three million homes for a year.

- Save water. Don't leave the water running while brushing teeth. Shut off garden hoses when not in use.

- Turn off lights in unused rooms.

- Turn off TVs when no one is watching.

- Save energy during the summer: Close shades or curtains to block out the hot sun. Use a fan instead of an air conditioner. Open windows for ventilation.

- Save energy during the winter: Open shades and curtains during the day to let the sun shine in. Close them at night to keep the heat inside. Wear a sweater at home or at the office, and turn the heat down to a lower setting.

- Recycle glass, plastic, paper, and metal.

- Reuse paper and plastic bags. Reusing saves natural resources. It also saves the energy that would be needed to make new products.

- When adults shop for home appliances, suggest that they read product labels to find out if the items are energy efficient.

Learn More Online

To learn more about greenscrapers, visit
www.bearportpublishing.com/GoingGreen

Glossary

architects (AR-ki-tekts) people who design buildings and manage their construction

compact fluorescent lightbulbs (KOM-pakt fluh-RESS-uhnt LITE-buhlbz) small lightbulbs that have a special energy-saving coating inside and can replace regular lightbulbs

conserve (kuhn-SURV) to stop something from being wasted

energy efficient (EN-ur-jee uh-FISH-uhnt) using as little energy as possible to operate

fiberglass (FYE-bur-*glass*) a material made of fine threads of glass

freshwater (FRESH-wa-tur) water that does not contain salt

fuels (FYOO-uhlz) things that are burned to produce heat or power

generators (JEN-uh-*ray*-turz) machines that produce electricity

global warming (GLOHB-uhl WORM-ing) the warming of Earth's air and oceans due to a buildup of greenhouse gases that trap the sun's heat in Earth's atmosphere

heat island effect (HEET EYE-luhnd uh-FEKT) higher temperatures in an area crammed with buildings and other human-made structures

incandescent lightbulbs (*in*-kan-DESS-uhnt LITE-buhlbz) glass containers holding a thin wire that gives off light when electricity flows through it; regular lightbulbs

insulation (*in*-suh-LAY-shuhn) something that prevents heat from escaping

limited (LIM-uh-tid) unable to increase

natural resources (NACH-ur-uhl REE-sorss-iz) materials found in nature, such as trees, water, and coal, that are useful to people

pollute (puh-LOOT) to release harmful substances into the environment

recycled (ree-SYE-kuhld) turned from something used, old, and unwanted into something new and useful

sensors (SEN-surz) devices that note the presence of something, such as heat or light

smog (SMOG) a mixture of fog and smoke caused by pollution

solar cells (SOH-lur SELZ) devices that can change energy from the sun into electrical energy

solar panels (SOH-lur PAN-uhlz) groups of solar cells that are connected to form flat boards or sheets

technology (tek-NOL-uh-jee) the science of making useful things

thermal chimney (THUR-muhl CHIM-nee) a large tube or shaft that lets warm air flow out of a building

ventilation (*ven*-tuh-LAY-shun) something providing fresh air to an indoor space

wind turbines (WIND TUR-byenz) machines that look like windmills and turn the power of the wind into electricity

Index

Bibliography

http://jetsongreen.typepad.com/jetson_green/skyscraper/index.html

www.buildinggreen.com/hpb/index.cfm

www.ecogeek.org/content/view/695/

www.ecoprojects.co.nz/Site/About/Principles_Of_Eco-Building.aspx

www.epa.gov/heatisland/index.htm

www.greenroofs.com/

Read More

Jefferis, David. *Green Power: Eco-Energy Without Pollution*. New York: Crabtree (2006).

Orme, Helen. *Climate Change*. New York: Bearport (2009).

Orme, Helen. *Living Green*. New York: Bearport (2009).

Sobha, Geeta. *Green Technology: Earth-Friendly Innovations*. New York: Rosen (2008).

About the Author

Steven L. Stern has more than 30 years of experience as a writer and textbook editor, developing books, educational products, and informational materials in a wide range of subject areas for children and adults. He is the author of 17 books as well as numerous articles and short stories. He has also worked as a teacher, a lexicographer, and a writing consultant.

WITHDRAWN